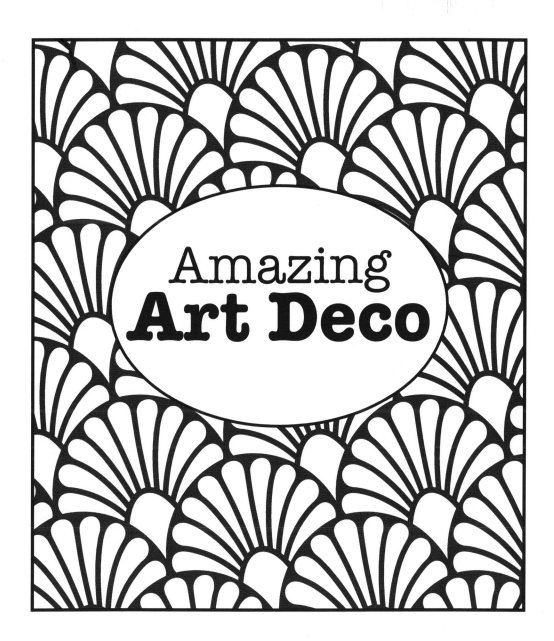

Amazing Art Deco

Really Relaxing Colouring **Book 8**

First published in 2015 by Kyle Craig Publishing

Text and illustration copyright © 2015 Kyle Craig Publishing

Editor: Alison McNicol

Design: Julie Anson

ISBN: 978-1-908707-93-2

A CIP record for this book is available from the British Library.

A Kyle Craig Publication

www.kyle-craig.com

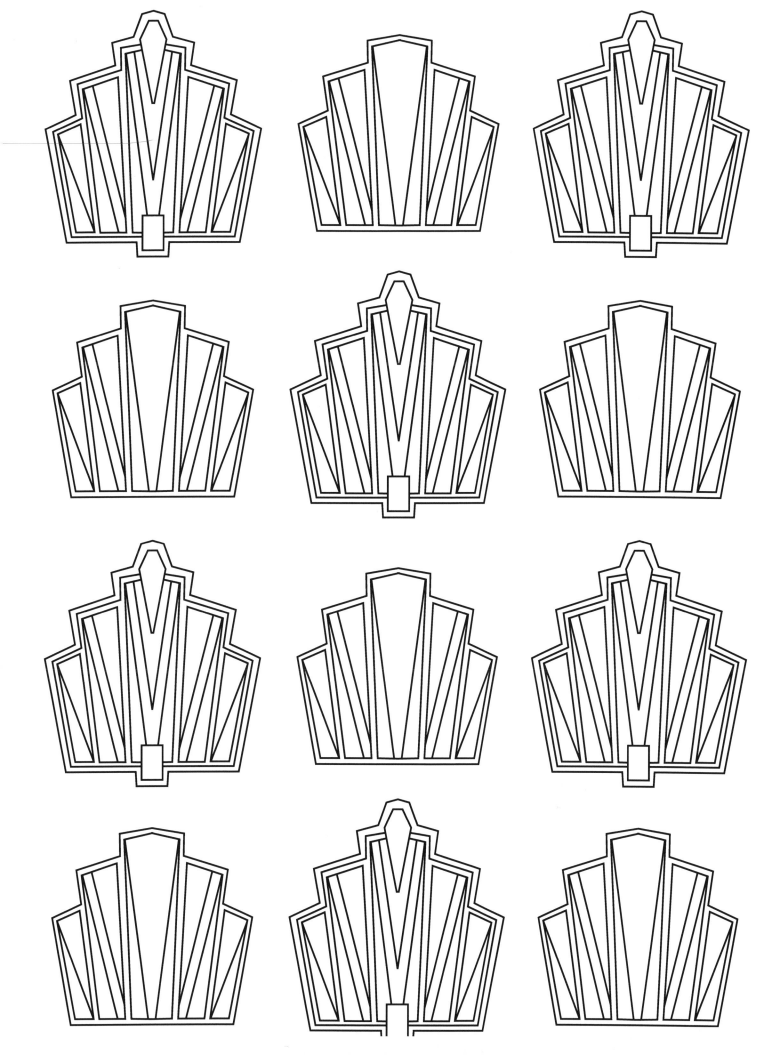

Printed in Great Britain
by Amazon.co.uk, Ltd.,
Marston Gate.